Life Cycles
and Reproduction

First published 2020
Foxton Books
London, UK

Copyright © Foxton Books, 2020

ISBN: 978-1-83925-010-1

Written by Nichola Tyrrell
Designed by Maryke Goldie
Logo design: Stewart Wright (2Wright Design)
Cover design: Ed White
Education consultant: Frances Barlow

About Foxton Primary Science:

The Foxton Primary Science series supports
Key Stage 1, Lower Key Stage 2 and
Upper Key Stage 2 Science.

This title supports the *Living Things and their
habitats* section of **Upper Key Stage 2**
through a variety of features and
STEAM-inspired tasks
that cover all curriculum requirements.

Colourful, engaging content blends
information with prompts
for further discussion and investigation.

Keywords, creative activities and quizzes
reinforce comprehension,
along with challenging words (in bold)
explained in the glossary.

Contents

Introduction

Once animals, including humans, are born, they get older and they grow. Many will reproduce and have babies themselves. Eventually, they will die. That is a life cycle.

As the babies reach adulthood, they too will often have their own offspring and the life cycle continues.

an emperor penguin family

Keywords adulthood life cycle reproduction

A similar cycle happens with plants, but instead of babies they make seeds or **spores**.

Dandelion seeds are blown by wind and will **germinate** elsewhere.

While animals and plants reproduce in different ways and with different life cycles, they are all working towards the same goal – to keep their species alive and well.

a warthog family

Life cycle: mammals

The life cycle of mammals, including humans, is similar for different species in several ways. Most mammal species give birth to live young. The young will grow to **resemble** their parents.

All mammal mothers have mammary glands to feed their offspring.

Some mammals have challenges and a different way of raising young. A kangaroo is a marsupial mammal that gives birth to undeveloped offspring. The size of a jellybean, blind and hairless, the baby joey will crawl into a pouch on its mother where it will stay for at least six months until it's fully formed.

Keywords mammal mammary gland marsupial

Life cycle: birds

Like mammal offspring, baby birds have the same body parts as their parents. The main difference is that chicks grow inside eggs. A **fertilised** egg grows into a chick by using nutrients in the yolk.

In many bird species, the parent birds take turns to sit on the eggs, **incubating** them until they are ready to hatch.

The bigger the egg, the longer it takes to hatch. An ostrich egg takes 42 days to hatch and it has the strongest of any shell – it can take a weight of up to 220 kilograms!

ostrich eggs

Once the hatchlings are born, usually without feathers, they stay in the nest until they are ready to fly.

Parents bring food to their growing young, now known as nestlings.

a robin hatchling

Over time, they practise flying until they can leave the nest, now fledglings.

mother hummingbird feeding hungry nestlings

Keywords   hatchling   nestling   fledgling

Life cycle: amphibians

Not all babies have the same body parts as their parents. Amphibians go through a life cycle that includes metamorphosis. This is the stage in a life cycle when the animal completely changes its body.

1. Frogs lay eggs in a clear jelly, called **frogspawn**, in a pond or on a wet leaf.

2. Each egg hatches into a tadpole, with a tail. It lives in water, breathing with gills. In a matter of weeks or months, it will grow legs and lose its tail.

3. Now fully grown, this European common frog is ready to spend time on land, breathing with lungs.

The female Suriname sea toad brings babies into the world in a different way. Her eggs attach and embed themselves into her back. They skip the tadpole stage completely and break through Mum's skin as fully developed frogs!

Keywords frogspawn metamorphosis

Life cycle: insects

Like amphibians, insects go through a stage of metamorphosis. Some have three stages, like the dragonfly that goes from egg to nymph to adult. Other insects have more work to do. They have four stages in their life cycle: egg, larva, pupa and adult.

A ladybird usually lays a **clutch** of tiny yellow eggs on the underside of a leaf, in the middle of an aphid colony. A week later, the eggs hatch and it becomes clear why they were laid amongst the aphids.

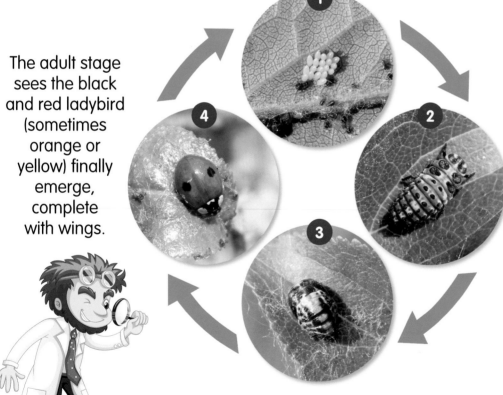

The adult stage sees the black and red ladybird (sometimes orange or yellow) finally emerge, complete with wings.

The eggs hatch into spikey black larvae that immediately start feeding on the aphids.

When fully grown, each larva changes again and seals itself into a yellow pupa. During this inactive stage, the biggest transformation takes place.

Keywords larva nymph pupa

Compare life cycles

Research the life spans of four different animals: a mammal, a bird, an amphibian and an insect.

Draw the life cycles for each animal, from egg to adult.

The life cycle of a bird might look like this:

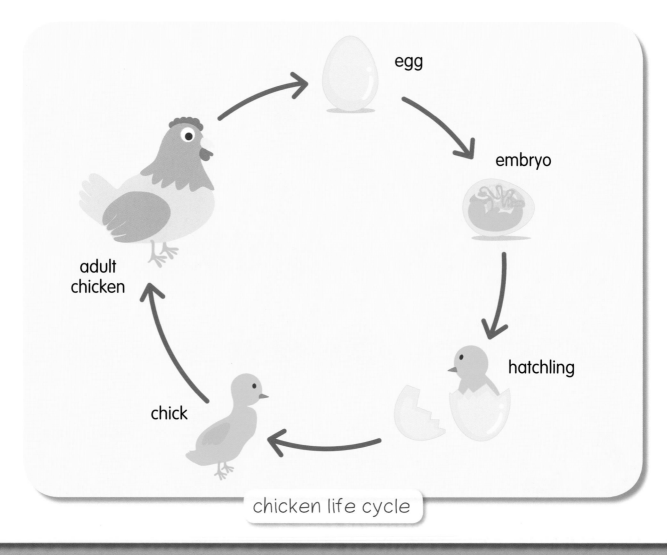

egg

embryo

hatchling

chick

adult chicken

chicken life cycle

The life cycle of
an amphibian might
look like this:

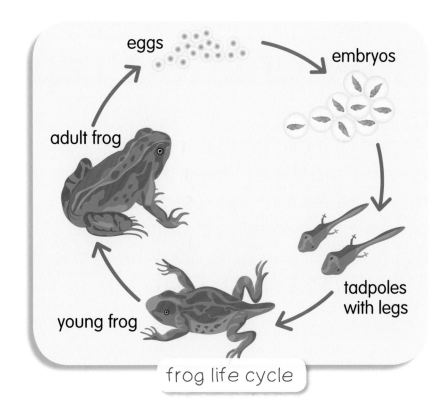

adult frog

eggs

embryos

tadpoles
with legs

young frog

frog life cycle

What similarities and differences are there between the life cycles?

Draw a bar chart that depicts the life span of all the animals. A bar chart
can show information vertically or horizontally.

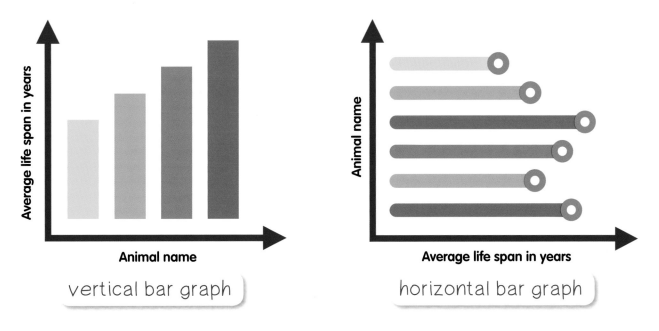

Average life span in years

Animal name

vertical bar graph

Animal name

Average life span in years

horizontal bar graph

Do you see a pattern?
Do you think the size of an animal affects its life span?

How animals reproduce

As part of their life cycle, plants and animals need to **reproduce** and make babies to keep their species alive. Most animals make babies through sexual reproduction by mating, with sperm from a male fertilising the egg of a female. This type of reproduction produces offspring that look similar to the parents but are not identical to them.

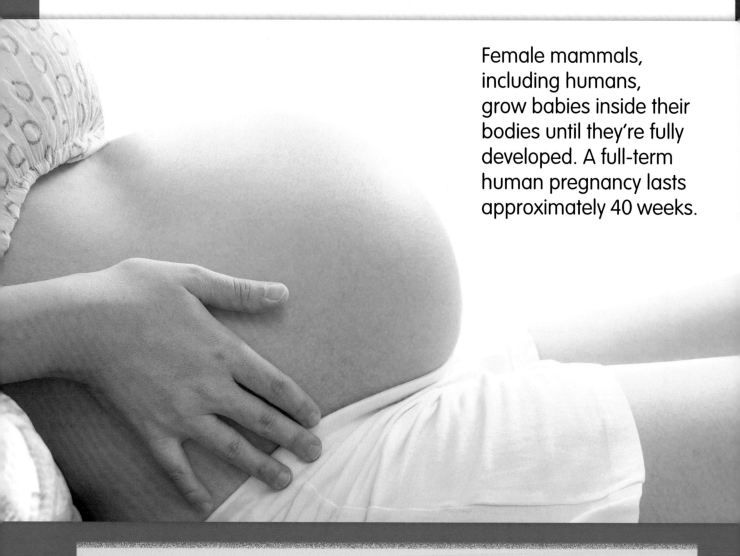

Female mammals, including humans, grow babies inside their bodies until they're fully developed. A full-term human pregnancy lasts approximately 40 weeks.

Keywords fertilise   pregnancy   sexual reproduction

Most aquatic animals fertilise eggs outside the female's body. Female salmon, for example, releases thousands of unfertilised eggs into the water that the male will fertilise.

little salmon fry keeping an eye on some eggs

eggs of a sea turtle, laid in a hole on the beach

Insects, birds and reptiles don't carry offspring. They lay fertilised eggs which will eventually hatch babies.

Madagascan hissing cockroach

Some animals, like the Madagascan hissing cockroach, carry their eggs internally. The eggs hatch as they are laid, making it resemble a live birth.

Assignment: Find out which two animals are the only mammals that lay eggs.

Comparing gestations

The gestation period is the length of time between the fertilisation of an egg and the birth of live young. In humans, we call this pregnancy. Gestations of different animals can vary greatly.

Research the gestation periods of mammals and compare them. Here are two to get you started:

For mammals, the longest known gestation is that of an elephant: nearly two years!

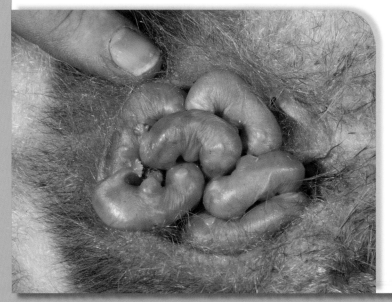

The opossum has the shortest mammal gestation period. It is pregnant for about 12 days and may birth up to 20 babies! Newborns crawl into Mum's pouch to keep warm and grow a bit more.

Draw a table similar to the one below to show the length of gestation for each mammal. Present the information as a bar chart, too. Turn to page 11 to find out more about making bar charts.

Animal:	Approximate gestation period (days):	Approximate gestation period (weeks):
Elephant	624	
Opossum	12	

Convert the gestation in days to weeks. Calculate this by dividing the gestation in days by 7.

Which animals have similar gestation periods?

Why do you think some animals have very long or very short gestations?

How plants reproduce

Like animals, plants start out small and grow until they are big enough to make plants of their own. Some plants reproduce sexually (with seeds and eggs) and others reproduce asexually (without seeds and eggs).

Asexual plants include those that are produced from **bulbs**, like tulips.

Keywords asexual bulb tuber vegetative reproduction

Asexual reproduction involves only one parent plant that can reproduce without an egg cell being fertilised to produce a seed. Instead, it makes an identical copy of itself.

Stages of vegetative reproduction from the leaf cutting of an African violet

When growing a plant from a cutting, it is **vegetative** asexual reproduction.

Plant **tubers**, like potatoes, are also asexual.

Like bulbs, tubers planted in soil will develop into new plants the following year.

Sexual plant reproduction

Plants that reproduce sexually do so through pollination. The flower produces pollen that insects or wind carry from the anther of one flower to the stigma of another flower.

honeybee with a large collection of pollen

Keywords fertilisation ovary pollination spore

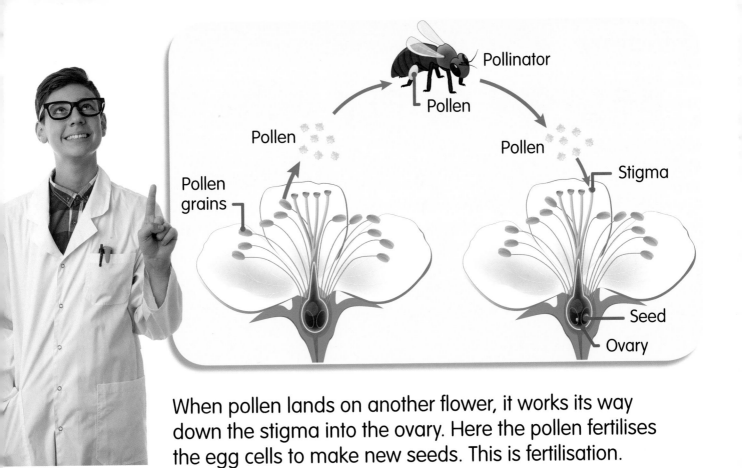

When pollen lands on another flower, it works its way down the stigma into the ovary. Here the pollen fertilises the egg cells to make new seeds. This is fertilisation.

Wind and animals, such as squirrels or birds, help to disperse the seeds to other locations where the seeds may **germinate** and grow into new plants.

Some non-flowering plants, like ferns and mosses, reproduce from tiny spores instead of seeds. The brown spots on a fern are spore casings. In time, the casings will dry out and the tiny spores inside will be blown away by wind, to settle elsewhere and germinate.

Regrow celery with cuttings

It's possible to force some plants to reproduce asexually by taking cuttings. Follow the steps below to grow celery from its roots. This method of asexual reproduction also works well with onions.

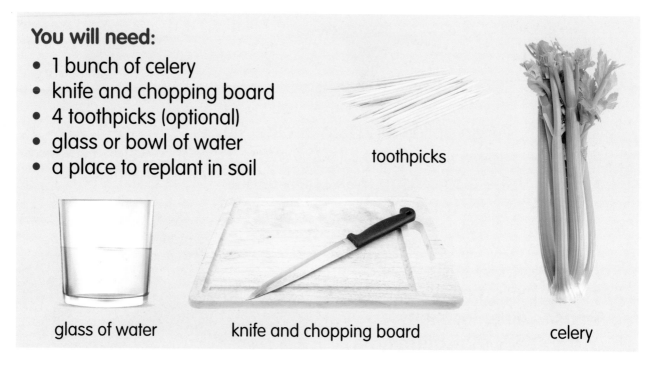

You will need:
- 1 bunch of celery
- knife and chopping board
- 4 toothpicks (optional)
- glass or bowl of water
- a place to replant in soil

toothpicks

glass of water

knife and chopping board

celery

1. With adult supervision, cut off the root end of the bunch, about 5 centimetres long.

2. Insert the toothpicks equally spaced around the root end, placed about 4 centimetres from the bottom. This is optional but may keep the outer layers from turning brown too quickly.

3. Place the root end in a bowl of water, about 8–10 centimetres deep and wide enough so the toothpicks are resting on the rim. Ensure the water covers about half the length of the root end.

4. Place the bowl in spot where it will receive natural light but not get too hot.

5. Change the water every other day, checking the bottom is submerged.

6. Within a few days, small leaves should sprout from the top.

7. After a week or so, small stalks and leaves may appear. At this stage, the cut stalks around the outside may be turning brown. This is a signal that it's time to plant the root end in soil.

8. You can plant the root end in a container or a garden outside. Choose an area that is shaded during the hottest part of the day.

9. For containers, use potting soil suitable for vegetables. Make a hole deep enough and big enough to fit the plant up to the cut end (but not covering it).

10. Keep the soil damp but not too wet. Celery can take about four months to fully grow its stalks. When ready, snap off the outer stalks and leave the inside ones to grow.

Produce a flap book

Write and design a flap book on a life-cycle topic of your choice. You could focus on the life cycle of a particular animal. You could write about a famous naturalist, such as David Attenborough or Jane Goodall. It's up to you.

Constructing the book:

- fold 3 × A3 size pieces of card in half and place one inside the other; this will give you ten inside pages plus front and back covers

- hole punch three holes 2 centimetres from the fold, at the top, middle and bottom; secure the pages together with string or wool through each hole

- make flaps by cutting smaller pieces of card to cover certain pictures; secure them with tape across the top (do this after the pictures are drawn or glued in)

Once you've chosen your topic, take the following steps to produce your book.

1. Prepare an outline. Plan a different subject for each page. Include a contents page and introduction at the beginning, and a glossary and index at the end.

2. Research and write the first draft of text.

3. Make a list of pictures; draw them or print them out.

4. Extra challenge: try to include as many keywords from this book as possible and include them in your glossary.

5. Write a second draft of text until you are happy with it. You may need to cut out parts if it's too long. Make sure your spelling, punctuation and grammar are correct.

6. Type your final text and print it out. Cut up paragraphs or chapters to glue into the book once you've constructed it.

7. Glue in your drawings or photographs and secure the flaps over top. You don't need to cover every image with a flap.

   Use different coloured tape or card for your flaps. They don't have to be square.

8. Finish with an eye-catching cover design and title!

Fruit fly life cycle

With a life span of just two weeks, the fruit fly is ideal for life-cycle observation. Set up conditions to encourage the reproduction of fruit flies and watch metamorphosis in action. Be warned: the rotting banana gets ugly!

You will need:

- an over-ripe banana
- an old jam jar
- a rubber band
- a magnifying glass
- kitchen paper

rubber band

banana

magnifying glass

paper towel

jam jar

1. Peel the banana and place it in an open jar outside.

2. In about two to six hours, tiny fruit flies should appear on the banana. If none appear, you can buy wingless fruit fly cultures from a pet shop.

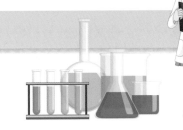

3. Cover the jar with a paper towel and secure it with a rubber band. You can now bring the jar indoors if you wish.

4. Use the magnifying glass to observe the fruit flies. Try to identify the males and females. Females are slightly larger with a pointy abdomen. Males have a larger black spot at the bottom of the abdomen.

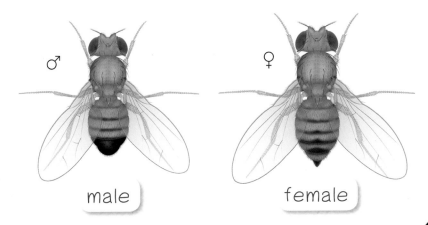

male   female

5. Check on the flies every day for ten days, recording observations daily.

fruit flies on a banana

Let's experiment (continued)

Draw or photocopy the chart below to record daily observations:

Life Cycle of Fruit Flies	
Observations:	
Day 1	
Day 2	
Day 3	
Day 4	
Day 5	
Day 6	
Day 7	
Day 8	
Day 9	
Day 10	

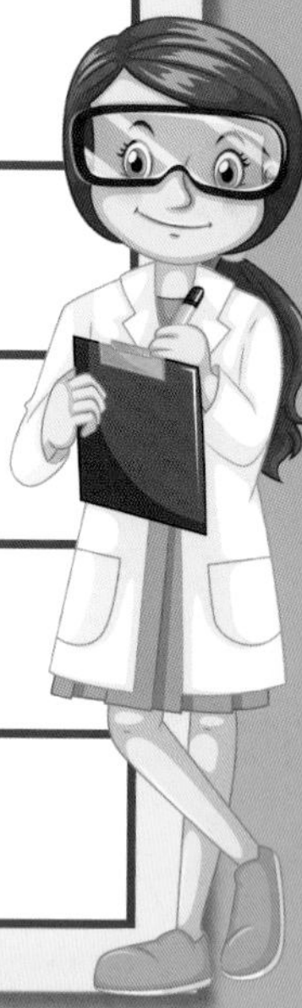

Predicted outcome

Stage 1: the fruit flies lay eggs

At first, tiny white dots should appear on the banana. These are eggs laid by the fruit flies.

Stage 2: the eggs change into larvae called maggots

Around day two or three, the eggs will turn into larvae – tiny wormlike maggots – that will start tunnelling into the banana as they eat it.

Stage 3: the larvae turn into pupae

Around day five, the maggots will attach themselves to the jar, forming structures that resemble grains of rice. These will darken in colour as the heads, legs and wings of the new flies grow.

Stage 4: new fruit flies develop

After ten days or so, a new generation of fruit flies should appear!

Did your flies perform as predicted? Did anything unexpected occur?

If you're happy to keep the jar for another ten days, the life cycle will repeat itself as the new flies mate and lay eggs.

fruit fly pupa

the same experiment using lemon

Comprehension check

1. Do most mammals lay eggs or give birth to live young?

2. What are the four stages of metamorphosis?

3. Which type of reproduction involves fertilising an egg: sexual or asexual?

4. For how many weeks do most human pregnancies last?

5. What powdery yellow substance do insects carry from flower to flower?

6. Which type of reproduction involves a single plant making a copy of itself?

7. Is a potato a tuber or a bulb?

8. Which group of animals fertilise eggs outside the female's body?

9. How can you regrow some vegetables such as celery without seeds?

10. Out of mammals, birds, amphibians and insects, which two groups have a life cycle that includes metamorphosis?

Turn to page 32 to mark your answers.

Vocabulary check

1. The stages of birth, growth, reproduction and death are known as a _ _ _ _ _ _ _ _ _ .

2. Many parent birds take turns to sit on their eggs, _ _ _ _ _ _ _ _ _ _ them until they are ready to hatch.

3. As part of their life cycle, plants and animals need to _ _ _ _ _ _ _ _ _ and make babies to keep their species alive.

4. Most animals make babies through sexual reproduction by mating, with sperm from a male _ _ _ _ _ _ _ _ _ _ _ the egg of a female.

5. The _ _ _ _ _ _ _ _ _ period is the length of time an animal is pregnant before giving birth or laying eggs.

6. Plants that reproduce sexually do so through _ _ _ _ _ _ _ _ _ _ .

7. Some non-flowering plants, like ferns and mosses, reproduce from tiny _ _ _ _ _ _ instead of seeds.

8. Taking cuttings is a method of _ _ _ _ _ _ _ reproduction.

9. _ _ _ _ _ _ _ _ _ _ _ _ _ is the stage in a life cycle when an animal completely changes its body.

10. Mammals have _ _ _ _ _ _ _ glands to feed their young.

Turn to page 32 to mark your answers.

Glossary

Definitions relate to the context of word usage in this book.

adulthood – the time of life when living being is grown up

asexual reproduction – reproduction by one parent only

bulb – a plant bud that starts to grow underground

egg – the female reproductive cell

fertilisation – the joining together of an egg and a sperm cell that develops into offspring

fertilise – to cause fertilisation of an egg

fledgling – a young bird that has grown feathers and has just learnt to fly

frogspawn – the eggs of a frog

germinate – to begin or cause growth

gestation – the time that an animal spends developing before its birth

gills – body structures that allow aquatic animals to take in oxygen from water

hatchling – a young animal that has recently left its egg

horizontal – parallel to the surface of the ground

larva – the wingless stage of an insect between hatching from its egg and becoming an adult

life cycle – the different stages of life of a plant or an animal

mammal – a warm-blooded animal with fur or hair, an interior skeleton, with milk-producing mothers

mammary gland – the organ of a female mammal that produces milk

marsupial – a type of mammal that carries undeveloped offspring in a pouch on its abdomen

metamorphosis – the change in body form during a life cycle

nestling – a newborn bird

nymph – a very young insect

ovary – in female animals, the part of the body that produces eggs; in a plant, the part where egg cells grow

pollen – the yellow powder made by a flowering plant

pollination – when wind or insects carry pollen from the flower of one plant to the flower of another plant

pregnancy – the gestation period whereby an animal grows young inside its body

pupa – an insect's stage of life after being a larva

reproduce – to make or have offspring

sexual reproduction – reproduction through the joining of an egg and a sperm from a female and a male

reproduction – the process of growing and having offspring

resemble – to look like or be similar to something

spore – a cell or group of cells that reproduce in some plants and animals

tuber – an underground plant stem

vegetative reproduction – asexual reproduction by plants

vertical – being upright

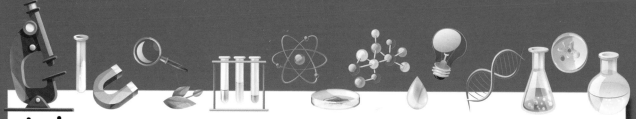

Index

Quiz answers

Comprehension check, page 28
1. give birth to live young
2. egg, larva, pupa, adult
3. sexual   4. forty   5. pollen
6. asexual   7. tuber   8. fish
9. take cuttings
10. amphibians and insects

Vocabulary check, page 29
1. life cycle   2. incubating
3. reproduce   4. fertilising
5. gestation   6. pollination
7. spores   8. asexual
9. metamorphosis
10. mammary

Photo credits

Shutterstock.com: cover: sezer66; pp. 1–2: Kazakova Maryia, balabolka, GraphicsRF; pp. 4–5: vladsilver, HHelene, Rudi Hulshof; pp. 6–7: Thuwanan Krueabudda, Jiri Haureljuk, GraphicsRF, mezzotint, Gabrielle Hovey, Ondrej Prosicky; pp. 8–9: AimoKinnas, Macrolife, Fotimageon, Dan Olsen, Kazakov Maksim, GraphicsRF; pp. 10–11: aekikuis, GraphicsRF (x2), snapgalleria, Macrovector; pp. 12–13: maradon 333, Zykov_Vladimir, ymgerman, Four Oaks; pp. 14–15: Nicolas Primola, Breck P. Kent, GraphicsRF; pp. 16–17: maoyunping, fotohunter, FotoDuets, Kazakova Maryia, Helder Almeida, pp. 18–19: sumikophoto, Marut Sayannikroth, NOPPHARAT STUDIO 969, Designua, exopixel; pp. 20–21: ALEX S, photosync, Pla2na, Patnaree Asavacharanitich, Lynn Maree Ross, Kamila Sankiewicz Photo, Apostle; pp. 22–23: Rido, SchubPhoto, GO DESIGN, Jeka, Dasha D; pp. 24–25: GraphicsRF, Roblan, Sergio Sergo, milart, Robuns, Cipariss, Feng Yu, Aldona Griskeviciene, SUPAPORNKH, exopixel; pp. 26–27: GraphicsRF (x2), Isis Medri, Pong Wira, Marek Velechovsky, nkula; pp. 28–29: Romolo Tavani; pp. 30–32: Belozersky, GraphicsRF, Macrovector